Toledo Rez
& Other Myths

Collected Poems

Thomas Parrie

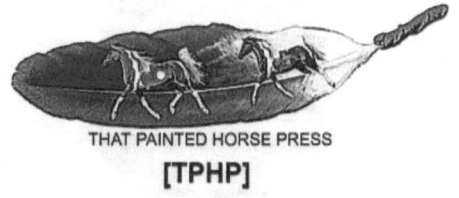

Harrah, Oklahoma
Calgary, Alberta
2019

Toledo Rez & Other Myths

© 2019 by Thomas Parrie

ISBN 978-1-928708-00-1

Except for fair use in reviews and/or scholarly considerations, no part of this book may be reproduced, performed, recorded, or otherwise transmitted without the written consent of the author and the permission of the publisher.

Cover Art: "Nuestra madre, nuestra tierra/Ishki pim, yakni pim" © 2019 Kiki Shawnee

Author Photo ©2018 Garret P. Vreeland with Array Design Studio

Editor: Rain Prud'homme-Cranford
Book Design: That Painted Horse Press
Cover Design: Rain Prud'homme-Cranford

Native Writers' Circle of the Americas

[IPLC]
Indigenous Publishers
Literary Collective

That Painted Horse Press: A Borderless Indigenous Press of the Americas
https://thatpaintedhorsepress.blogspot.com

Acknowledgements

"Indian Morphology" and "Quetzalcoatl in Louisiana" *Excavating Honesty: An Anthology of Rage and Hope in America. Paper Nautilus*, 2016.
"The Great Flood." *Rabbit and Rose*, 2016.
"Alligator Gar and Other Poems" *The Southern Quarterly*, 2016.
"Memorials" *Four Winds Literary Magazine*, 2015.
"Dog Head Park" *Codex Journal*, Pushcart Prize Nominee, 2014.
"Anthropology" *Codex Journal*, 2014.

Lyrics

"Mathilda" Cookie and the Cupcakes. *Kings of Swamp Pop*, 1959
"Come and Get Your Love" Redbone. *Wovoka*, 1973.
"Don't Fear the Reaper" Blue Oyster Cult. *Agents of Fortune*, 1976.

Table of Contents

Dedication	iii
Preface	iv

I. Part I: Rez Myths Resurfaced

Quetzalcoatl in Louisiana	3
The Story of Drowning Bear and Mud Turtle	4
In the Hills, the Flowers	5
Sasquatch Woman	6
Fat Choctaw-Apache Jesus	7
One Culled Down	8
The Story of Two Lost Indians	9
Indian Justice System	10
Bottle Rocket Barbeque	11
1967 Word Series	12
The Old Man and His Fence	13
The Story of the Warrior Snake	14

II. Part II: In Memoriam of the Traditional

Indian Morphology	16
Alligator Gar	18
Outside Broken Bow, OK	19
Aunt Ruby's Burial Flag	20
Dog Head Park	21
Johnny NoCasino's Missing Arm	22
Anthropology	23
Animals Remember for Us	24
Memorials	25
Notes on a Christian Children's Fund Commercial in 1992	27
You Got Some New Used Boots	28
I Knew an Indian From Colorado Once	29
I Know a Woman Who Swears She Once Met Geronimo in Walmart in 1983	30

III. Part III: Dancing to Remember, Dancing to Forget

When the Parrie Boys Cover Redbone 32
When Joe Crow Taught Us how to Play Our Homemade Guitars 33
Wolfman Jack Takes Callers During an Interview with the Parrie Boys on KRLA Pasadena 34
Elegies from the Backseat of a Pontiac 35
Charlie Goodtime 37
Friday Night at Coon Ridge Bar 38
Saturday Night at Coon Ridge Bar 39
When Columbus Discovers America, Again 40
Snow High Enough 41
Moon Ridge Drum Song 42
Chief's Two Left Shoes 43
I Don't Bless People when they Sneeze 44
Portrait of a Velvet Indian Elvis 45

IV. Part IV: Yakni hupia, Oka hupia

Stomping Grounds 48
The Great Flood 49
One Artifact 50
Elegy for a Drowned 1969 Camaro 51
The Parrie Boys Run Out of Gas in Norman, OK 52
Graduation Ceremony 53
La Malinche Weeps 54
Beast Kings, 3rd Infantry Division 55
Gift Hour 56
My Father's Horses 57
Dry Summer Bone 58
Toledo Rez 59

Dedication:

The Toledo Bend Dam Project created one of the largest man-made freshwater reservoirs in west Louisiana and east Texas. It is known to house the largest catfish and bass in the south, a veritable sportsman's paradise. In order to create it in the late 1960s, the federal and state government dammed the Sabine River, flooding thousands of acres of unrecognized Indian land on the border between Louisiana and Texas. The people living there relocated to the shores while some moved away for good. What was left behind still sits at the bottom of the lake.
For the Choctaw-Apache of Ebarb Community

Preface

I came to this project while at McNeese State University's MFA program. For years, it was just a title and a few fledgling poems that had made it through the rigorous workshop. I'd grown tired of them, tired of poetry, but I kept coming back to them because of what they represent.

The lines, the images herein, echo to me the way culture and language echoes to my father. When I visit him (which is less these days than I'd like), the memories and stories he has of growing up in Sabine Parish resurface, and he delights in retelling to me the stories of his time. These are the stories of being Choctaw-Apache, of being Indigenous.

It would take him thirty years or so before someone would hand him a tribal ID card with his name on it saying that *being a Parrie meant being an Indian* — An identity that he'd been denied for so long, always being misidentified and mislabeled as Latino. My father spent his life being Native, a lot of times not being able to prove it to the outside world or to himself, but an identity he nonetheless reclaimed, much like the tribe itself.

Toledo Rez & Other Myths is about displacement in body and in soul. It is about reclaiming what has been taken, what has been denied, whether it was land, language, or tradition, or all the above. Most importantly, this collection is about taking what's left and making something new, something that breathes, that walks and talks, something that dances and remembers. And while some of the stories included are fiction, this book represents the real families of the Choctaw-Apache Tribe of Ebarb, Louisiana, and is dedicated to them.

~ Thomas Parrie, Hammond, La., 2019

I. Rez Myths Resurfaced

Quetzalcoatl in Louisiana

was discovered in the woods along a deer trail
        (stretched the width of the 6 foot path).
They threw beer cans at it from the truck cab

while mocking its indigo plumage, its bird caw language.
        They loaded their Winchester repeating rifles
and turned front wheels to grind it into earth.

They could not identify its species.
        Could be cottonmouth, copperhead, sun god,
or some other kind of river swimmer.

So they readied their dragging chains
        and, just to be sure, called in the 7th Cavalry Regiment.
Quetzalcoatl opened its mouth to speak, but swallowed the woods around them.

So, they flooded its homelands and bought
        lake front property so they could charge it to live there,
then plucked out its feathers turning them into dreamcatchers.

They crushed its head with a rock to save their children
        from skin so dangerous, so dark,
but two more heads grew in its place.

And when the old dragon opened its mouths,
        crazy with its own venom,
it tore out its heart as an offering.

The Story of Drowning Bear and Mud Turtle

Once there was a bear who came upon a giant lake in what had been his hunting ground. The bear sniffed around the water, but didn't recognize any of the scents. He then decided to enter the water and cross to the other side. But as the water rose, he felt his mighty paws slipping on the slick lake bottom as a great current swept him over, and pulled him beneath the water. The bear tried to yell for help, but all that came out was a mighty roar that scared away all the fish and beaver. But just as he was about to drown, he felt the slick lake bottom move up and up until the bear was standing on a small island in the middle of the lake. The island began to move toward the bank, carrying the soggy bear to land. When he reached the shore, the bear was shocked to see that a turtle had saved his life. The turtle had been sleeping in the mud at the bottom of the lake and awoke just as the bear began to drown. The bear then asked, "What do I owe you for saving my life?" To which the turtle replied, "I sleep here every year and every year another great black bear drowns here. This year, I figured I would save your life so that next year when I come out of the water, you won't eat me. So, if you want to repay me, just don't forget that the turtle saved your life." So, every year when the turtle appears from the mud, the bear dances on the bank, celebrating his long life.

In the Hills, the Flowers

> Most American Indian slaves seem to have been women and children
> most of whom were baptized and raised in the European communities
> —Hiram "Pete" Gregory

Nights beyond the hamlets and groves of Toledo
Bend, moonflowers bloom over unmarked graves. Yielded
of petal and skin, of leaf and soul, not ghosts,
but memory faded to nature. Of mothers,

absolved *in articula mortis*, who were horse
and plow when alive, now plant and root along hills
and ridges, creek beds, and ditches, crook to wind gusts
as vines swaddle savage, unbaptized babes where she,

La Llorona, enters this world to take their souls.
There is a release when she cups them, holds them close
to her bone skin. Then blooms close with the falling dawn,
leaving behind the scent of fresh Easter lilies.

In the hills, new flowers will pit as seed, and vine
to bloom, to grow and spread over the potter's field.

Sasquatch Woman

Even on her death bed,
she claimed finding her baby
Bigfoot in '64 and nursing
him back to health.
She fed him tomatoes.
He loved chasing egrets.

She taught him to say *oka*
and *hoshi*. The day she let him go
was the day she lost her son.
Not like she would in '74
to a bullet, orphaned
in the blue gunner dark.

Her baby Bigfoot came back
in the summer of '84 with his
own baby Bigfoot, and they ate
tomatoes with her on her porch
beneath their swamp moon.
When she got too old, she

was moved to a home where
she told nurses angels sat with her
at night, she could hear her ancestors
singing while she slept, and her baby
bigfoot watched over her
through her third floor window.

Fat Choctaw-Apache Jesus

looks like a Buddha, but I bet
no one has ever set themselves on fire for him.

has a beard like Santa Claus, but
we all know crows live in it.

followed us home from the store one winter
and gave us tamales and Hot Pockets.

left a trail of corn shucks and cardboard sleeves
that vanished into the carpet when the sun hit them.

is the Energizer Bunny of Jesuses. After he dies,
he can still get drunk on his own blood.

> And god, do we confess all our sins to him,
> as if he could part the sea for us.

He's a train hurdling through indigenous darkness
and we ride on top of it.

We ride inside of it, laying as planks
to keep it chugging, to never get left behind.

One Culled Down

from across the red gravel road

   where six white egrets fly low

      in the mist over the field

         where one drops under

      line of sight

   beneath the weeds

beside the pasture

The Story of Two Lost Indians

Two got lost in the woods and wandered for most of the day until they came upon a chief who invited them into his home. When he saw their baggy clothes, he gave them tobacco. When he saw their dry mouths, he showed them pictures of his ancestors. And when they were ready to go back into the woods, the chief gave the first one his son's Vietnam Service Medal. And then he turned to the second one and gave him a bundle of sage and said, "If you split this in half, you can share with your brother." He then led them out, and as they entered the forest, the chief began to sing and shake his gourds. Later, the two lost Indians threw away the sage and traded the medal for Spam and Evan Williams.

Indian Justice System

The first murder happened when a warrior killed another warrior of the same village. After the funeral, all the mothers gathered in the center of the village where the old chief stabbed the ground with a spear. Leaving the spear in the ground, he said that whoever killed the warrior would appear in front of the spear the next morning. When morning came, the people saw that the murderer standing in shame next to the spear was the old chief's son. The old chief walked up to his son and asked if he killed the warrior, to which the son said, yes. All the mothers gathered around the spear, the old chief, and his son. Then the old chief took out his knife and slit his son's throat.

Bottle Rocket Barbeque

Fireworks explode over us in the parking lot
of the fire station as kids chase each other
with roman candles, shooting fireballs like bullets,
and we yell with them more than we yell at them.

Cracking booms lift the night in glittery fizzle-gold
as sparks fall over cars and over Big Warren, asleep
in backseat of his mother's old Pontiac.
Through rocket shriek and popping black cats you hear,
Lettemsleepitoff.   We light more fuses,

more hand grenades, more round shells, more
warheads. Smoke from cooling charcoals mingles
with sulfur and ozone and we round dance
in the haze of fire and flesh.

Big Warren hugs his knees closer to his chest,
while kids play war, we gather around our cars.
We take stock of potato salad, baked beans,
and how to divide what's left of the meat.

1967 World Series

"was *the impossible dream,*

that he could just walk home from Vietnam,

walk right through the door and ask

for supper even after they had said *friendly fire,*

said *misguided air targets,*

but there he was in our kitchen,

smaller than a corn stalk,

and wanting to eat, and the six of us running

to him like *we* had won the series."

The Old Man and His Fence

A long time ago there was this old Indian who lived in a house with a white picket fence. And every day that he tended his corn, he would find parts of his fence missing or broken. And every day, he would mend it back. Sometimes, animals would sneak through the fence to eat his corn, and the old man would shoo them away by running out on his porch and waving his arms. One day he noticed a group of wild Indians standing by his fence staring at his house. Before he could shoo them away, they asked for food and water while on their way to Oklahoma. The old man remembered a story someone told him about how wild Indians would ask for food and water only to leave and come back asking for more and more. Sometimes, it was a trick and they would rob and kill them. The old man raised his arms to shoo them away and one of the them pulled a knife, so the old man pulled up a piece of broken fence and hit him and bashed in his head. The rest scattered and never came back.

The Story of the Warrior Snake

A long time ago there was an Indian village that had become surrounded by enemy warriors. These enemy warriors laid siege to the village for weeks until one day, one of the village warriors said, "Let's go fight them! And if we die, we die in battle!" And so they charged the enemy with all their might, except for one who turned himself into a snake and slithered into a basket and fell asleep. When he woke, still a snake, he found that all of the people had died and interstates and skyscrapers had replaced his village. This made him very angry, and so he began biting everyone he saw, and when he did, they all turned back into Indians.

II. In Memoriam of the Traditional

Indian Morphology

Chusca (choo-ska) – Buzzard

Aunt Ruby calls me over and points at birds
circling over the creek. She tells me something is dead
or will die soon.

Pichicuate (peachy-coo-atay) – Water Moccasin

I can't swim in the creek,
so I jump in the Atlantic and swim all the way to Spain.
I have some grievances.

Jicote (heco-tay) – Wasp

Remember when I was allergic to their sting? Remember when I fell
on that nest and they stuck me nine times? Dad, you told me
not to go to sleep cause I might die.
You've called me *Jicotalito* ever since.

Cuate (koo-watay) – Twin

We avenge our fathers and uncles through baseball games. And when we
win, brothers, which we always do, we become the sun and the moon.
This is always the beginning of a new age.

Nixtamal (neex-tamal) – Boiled Corn

Gods used to hide in the rows behind the house and wait
for me to fall asleep. Then, they would sneak into my room,
reach out their husk covered hands, and touch my dreams,
in which I'm holding a dagger.

Cacahuate (kaka-hoo-atay) – Peanut

Sometimes the peanut butter and the jelly came mixed

in the same jar. You told me the peanut was magical.
It was our buffalo.

Chichimec (meco/a) (chee-chee-mec) – Indian Pejorative

You put mud and cobwebs on our scrapes.
You made fish hooks out of beer cans.
You made us chew boiled sweet gum tree for toothaches.
You taught us that cedar kept away the fleas.
We told other kids we didn't know you.

Chichi (chee-chee) – Mother's Milk

Two fight over a six-pack
of Old Milwaukee. One stabs the other
in the back. The stabbed one keeps drinking
with the knife still in his back
until he bleeds out.

Cuacha (kwaa-cha) – Shit

Hey cousin, we used to steal bicycles from white kids
and ride them all the way to the next town.
They were our ponies.
And we had many.

Chonche (chaan-chee) – Slave

In Choctaw it meant "wild bird."
In Caddo it meant "bondage."
In Choctaw-Apache it meant 200 years of hiding and blending in.
We don't speak the language, but we know
what it means when we see buzzards.

Alligator Gar

After we caught the damned thing,
we stretched it out on the nearest picnic table.
The creature's back was the same deep Toledo
Bend brown we all birthed and owned.

From snout to tail, it took up the whole table.
Its belly was pale and protruded full of fish.
Scales casted off the daylight in rainbows that caught
the eye in moments of its writhing.

A half-breed: not quite alligator, not quite fish.
In life, this must have driven it crazy.
Its amber-foil eyes popped like tin cans
watching us take it apart.

Watching the irreverent swash of the lake,
watching my uncles pry open its red ribbon gills,
slicing their hands as they entered its folds.
Watching my father cut his fingers on the dorsal fin,

bathing it in Indian blood as it cracked its
bone-knife jaws against the alien air.
Then my grandfather shoved his hand into
its long mouth and pulled out the hook.

I saw its meat ripple beneath their grip in waves.
I saw prayers float like air bubbles the day
we killed the alligator gar.

Our brown and bleeding hands mingled
with the brown back of the lake.
Each one of us ensnared between the heavy sky
and those eyes, as ancient and hazy as our names.

Outside Broken Bow, OK

On the first night you took us to the big powwow,
I lay in the back of our truck, my face
as big as the moon from the fists of a Cheyenne kid
who didn't like my white mom.

Hey breed! and *Go back to your apple tree!*
had found me in Indian country without a green card.
Without a rez card. Without my skin.
Where we came from, Indians weren't this real.

They were dollar store Indian.
They were Wounded Knee Indian.
They were chicken-feather-roach-clip Indian.
Then in the parking lot, you said, *ya, jicotalito,*

we're In-dyun too while holding in joint smoke.
You kept me awake after my battle.
Told me I could die if I feel asleep, told me
In-dyuns don't die in their sleep. Handed me a beer

for taking my first fist to the face.
Blood from my busted lip settled at the back
of my throat as I breathed in fumes, drums,
and smoke. We sat in the parking lot

around a boom box until night came
with its revving V8 dynamos,
arena light aurora,
and our dumb luck, and wild eye.

Aunt Ruby's Burial Flag

sits on her table next to her Jesus figurine.
And when you're in her kitchen, she'll tell you
the tamale was once an offering to the gods.
They were as essential as a warriors beating heart.
They are the dead wrapped and put in an earthen pit
to rise and feed thousands. They were as vital
as a woman's living heart stuffed into shuck and steamed.
She'll place a plate of stacked tamales in front of you,
on her kitchen table, next to her burial flag, and her statue
of Jesus who opens his arms as wide as most open their mouths.

Dog Head Park

When he gets drunk, Larry tries to kill himself
because he says he would rather die in battle
than grow old, but we all know
he stole the line from *War Party*,

> (in which the Indian heroes charge
> the national guard with tomahawks
> and clubs they stole from a museum).

One time, he got his ass kicked in a fight he started
when he came upon a group of drunks in the woods
and attacked them with a log. He said they fought
like dogs and their teeth

> were as white and foul as the stars and tore
> off most his skin that will never grow back.
> They left him to die in the brush and the mud.

One time, when we were all drinking
he told us our ancestors ate their dogs.
And that they deserved to be conquered,
so we tore off the rest of his skin.

Johnny NoCasino's Missing Arm
after Natalie Diaz

Johnny NoCasino sits on the same barstool every day
swilling whiskey water and complaining about arthritis
in the arm he doesn't have. He tells women it was chopped
off by Osama Bin Laden himself and is now a trophy
behind museum glass, or floating in a vat of saline,
or stuffed and mounted on the wall of some hut,
but everyone knows he lost it when he was ran over
by a log truck when he was seven, but we don't say anything.

Sometimes, a woman will dance with him
or she'll buy him a whiskey water, but most of the time
he drinks until he slides off the barstool, then bow-legs
back to his bullet trailer in the morning.

Once a woman went home with him, but we could tell
she would have rather gone home with the arm
he doesn't have—the artifact clenched in a fist forever.

Anthropology

Wild horses gather at midnight around
the fire of the local bar where they drink
from trough beer and talk crazy dreams in a
language even they can't understand. When
they tell us their stories, they punctuate
them with hoof beats. They look for broken twigs.
They speak broken English. When sun comes,
their carcasses are eaten by buzzards.
After bones are cleaned, skeletons
sink into prairie grass to be dug up
by anthropologists who glue and stitch
and wire them back together. In order
to preserve horse culture, they save the bones
and sell them back to the horses at midnight.

Animals Remember for Us
–for Mike, who laughs

The night you shot yourself at your mother's,
I was locked out of my house again, so I slept
on the porch, and woke from the cold to see
a tar-eyed buck in a grove of baby pines,
snapping bark like an antlered albatross.

A possum carried pups on her back.
Waddling through the yard, watching me,
she curled her tail, and dipped her head
into the dark. I fell back asleep
amid the distant caw of a ringing phone.

Memorials

They said the cross was fifty feet high, and twenty five feet across,
and made from steel and copper as thick as two pennies,

the same stuff the statue of liberty is made of.
It was in honor, they said, to those modern warriors who died

fighting for the red, white, and blue. So, one night,
when the moon had turned away, we hooked the back of my old Grand Cherokee

to its base and tried to pull it down, but ended up breaking the axle instead,
so we abandoned my truck, and walked home promising

to never say a word. No one moved the beat up thing, and as months passed,
hardly anyone came out to visit the cross until,

one Easter morning, they found Big Warren's body in the driver's seat
covered in a Pendleton blanket and missing his shoes.

After this, they towed the truck to a wrecking yard,
and had his service around the cross.

He was one of those who died long after his war ended. He was
a member of the fallen off barstools tribe. Those who, pissing themselves,

danced through the night like ghost dancers bringing back the buffalo.
Vets of Toledo Rez who traded their purple hearts for pain killers and speedballs.

Who set up tipi's in parking lots of liquor stores singing
"Matilda, I cried and cried for you. I want my baby back again!"[1]

---

[1] Cookie and the Cupcakes. "Mathilda." *Mathilda*, Judd Records, 1957.

The cross still stands with us in the shadows of Jesus and Mary.
Shadows of death and dancing. Shadows

of elders holding hands around its base
like flags for fallen brothers.

Shadows for a landscape of ruin.
For broken axles and beer bottle memorials.

Notes on a Christian Children's Fund Commercial in 1992

I tell my father we should consider
sponsoring one of those kids. I tell him
the old dude on TV says they'll send
us the picture of a kid with a message
about their family. I tell him for the price
of a cup of coffee, he could give a kid a break.
I tell him I imagine having a new brother
or sister and he stops me and says
why should he support all the horse-eyed kids
on TV when he already has one at home.

That I look like the Lone Ranger
because I never clean the dirt from my eyes.
That we shop junkyards and pick
from the city dump too, and all we get
are census takers and anthropologists,
yearning to save us from Walmart parking lots
and everyday low prices. The only miracle
he ever saw was when the Army
set up a recruitment office next to the Texaco.
He tells me to go back to my video games

but I don't have any. When Joe Crow comes,
he tucks us under his wing. He drops us
from the clouds. And we end up landing
in the jungles and in the deserts, feet first,
back into the ground.

You Got Some New Used Boots

Your mama made you mocs
and you traded them for a horse.
Ride, baby, ride until that horse breaks,
then trade it for some boots.
And wear those boots

in snowy Rapid City streets,
in thickets and prairies,
on brick-topped Jackson Square
beneath ol' green horse.

Wear those boots through canyon
and river, along bleeding Juarez streets,
through planet and moon. Run

toward the sun and the hole in the sky.
Keep running baby, they wanna kill you.

I knew an Indian from Colorado Once

You sold me out for a dozen white women
and a warm place to sleep. You shaved your head
and went to war against me, with the mountains,

with Denver. You shake your fist at the snow
while standing in the road holding wild flowers
and sloughing off dead skin. How you move
from town to town searching for places to sleep,

too drunk to pay the bills, too stupid
to do anything, but howl into the sun.

I Know a Woman Who Swears She Once Met Geronimo in Walmart in 1983

The old man was at the snack bar drinking coffee and reading the paper when she urged her grandson to ask, "Are you him?" He took a sip of coffee. "Yep, I'm him," he said, not looking at them. "Can you say something?" "Yep," he said, "I can speak every language. As a matter of fact, I know every word that has ever been said." After a few minutes the boy said, "Okay, if you know every word, prove it." The grandmother pinched her grandson, but he wasn't fazed. The old man put down his paper. After a long breath, he gestured his arm away from his chest and said, "ya-at-tey." The kid repeated him, "e-yaaa-tahey," and the old man corrected him, saying it again while waving his arm. The grandmother asked, "What does it mean?" "It means 'may the Great Spirit be with you,'" he said to her. Then he looked to the boy, "whenever someone asks who you are, you can tell them that." The boy repeated this new magical incantation, memorizing it so he could unveil it to the kids at school and mesmerize them with his authentic words. Then the old man leaned forward and looked dead into his eyes and said, "It also means bad motherfucker."

III. Dancing to Remember, Dancing to Forget

When The Parrie Boys Cover Redbone

we feel
the bending string,

hey-ya, hey-ya,
what's the matter with ya,
don't ya feel right, baby?[2]

You stand
at the bar
and order me flowers,

come and get your love.[3]

Say the beer
makes them sound better,
makes the chords ring truer,

and I will dance,
slow, pushed against you,
against your open chest,

against the hangover morning.
You against the Army,
your rifle tucked

in your back pocket.
My arms around your neck,
a cigarette between my fingers.

Your leather jacket.
Others can bite bullets,
we will never stop dancing.

---

[2] Redbone. "Come and Get Your Love." *Wovoka*, Lolly Veges, Epic Records, 1973.
[3] Ibid.

When Joe Crow Taught Us How to Play Our Homemade Guitars

A long time ago there were four brothers who forgot how to speak. So they made themselves guitars out of the wood from an ash tree. They made strings from deer sinew. They made their pics from the chips of the mud turtle shell. They spoke only by playing their guitars, but no one could understand them until one day, Joe Crow came to the brothers, led them into the hills, and showed them some chords. His guitar was made of the sharpest obsidian and the finest silver. His strings were made from gold. He left the brothers in the woods for three days. And when the brothers came back to their village with their new way of talking, they began to play on their homemade guitars, playing the songs Joe Crow had taught them. Suddenly, all the people began to dance and speak to each other in their new language.

Wolfman Jack Takes Callers During an Interview with The Parrie Boys on KRLA Pasadena

WOLFMAN: *Who's ready to hear the sound coming from down South Louisiana on a Tuesday night?*

    CALLER 4: No way, you guys are really Indians?

PARRIE BOYS: No, I mean, yes, but we're a band, you know?

    CALLER 6: I ain't never seen an Indian before 'cept TV and one time my boyfriend was Geronimo for Halloween. I was Pocahontas.

    CALLER 3: Do y'all play *Indian* music?

PARRIE BOYS: We're a rock band.

WOLFMAN: *And are you all brothers?*

PARRIE BOYS: Um, no, we're cousins, some of us.

    CALLER 9: I saw them in Hollywood last night at '71 and they were really cool.

    CALLER 5: They're super sexy. I just want to run my fingers their hair!

WOLFMAN: *And that's the heart and soul of rock n roll, baby,*
we got music from a band of brothers 'cause we
all brothers tonight. Hey guys out there keep the love in your heart, baby
'cause next up, we got The Parrie Boys live in the studio on this Tuesday night.
I know it's raining outside, but that's all the more reason to stay tuned.
Let's give the boys a minute to warm up, so how about some
Skynrd on KRLA Pasadena!

Elegies from the Backseat of a Pontiac
after Adrian C. Louis

I
The last few weeks before we left for basic
we went turkey hunting with my dad.
He would end up leading the song at your funeral.
Another beer and I remember him talking about 'nam.
Another beer and you ain't dead.
Another goddamn miracle! Another round.
That was the day he finally told us about the woman
and her kid he found in the rice granary
when a flock of turkeys burst right over our heads
pelting us with wing feathers.

II
When I heard about you, I went to see your sisters.
And I want to tell you that we sang songs for you.
And I want to tell you that we said prayers for you.
And that we got drunk in your name,
in the name of the saints,
in the name of the martyrs.

III
I remember Dad laughing at us because we were scared
of the turkeys. Because they looked like cartoons. Hell,
we looked like cartoons.

IV
Last night I saw your death and I heard
your funeral song but I was mainlining in Shreveport,
getting arrested in Tulsa, losing my scalp in California,
still running from Fallujah.

V
Drink another and you're a corpse in a rearview mirror
hitching a ride with me when I sleep in strange backseats.
Where they taking us, cousin?

> *All our times have come*
> *here, but now they're gone*[4]

Can you hear me?
When I wake from this stupor,
and the next?

---

[4] Blue Oyster Cult. "(Don't Fear) The Reaper." *Agents of Fortune*, Columbia Records, 1976.

Charlie Goodtime

sits Indian style in middle
of dance club with his peace
pipes and his ayahuasca roots
promising all the babes one way
trips to heaven.
Tells them there's good medicine
in his finger bone rattles. Knows
the best trails to sacred mounds
where he loots graves to sell
parts along with hemp ropes
and dreamcatchers
to all the pretty girls.

Friday Night at Coon Ridge Bar

"This ain't the Wild West, but we make do," the old man says, "this is where I came before Korea. And I fell in love with Darla right out there on the sawdust. Shipped out the next day, and when I came back, I learned she'd died, got shot somewhere in Texas. So, I married her sister." He shows me the bullet lodged in the center of a tattoo that reads *Darla* on his chest. "That's not from Korea," he laughs, "that's from her sister."

Saturday Night at Coon Ridge Bar

"Let me get something straight," the old woman says, "there ain't no reservation here, we never lived on one. There's a reservoir and we've lived around it since they built it. Before that, we lived right in the middle of it." She leans on the bar and picks up a shot glass. "Got those damned dogs though. That's why there ain't no more panthers round here." She takes the shot. "Those mangy bastards sleep under cars all day and then sit on your couch and demand to eat." She lights a cigarette. "Shit, they'll even let you pet'em until they get to drinking. That's when they bite."

When Columbus Discovers America, Again

he ambles through the doors of our house,
and asks for water,

        then bread,
                then blood.

When Columbus discovers our powwow,
he crawls to the center of our circle,
and plants a flag,

        then a cross,
             then gallows,
                      then a federal holiday.

When Columbus discovers our music,
he bellies up to the bar,
and demands the bar,

        then the woods,
            then the lakes,
                  then the planet.

When Columbus discovers America, again,
he wears feathers and war paint,
and calls us brothers,

        then Indians,
        then savages,
              then mascots.

Snow High Enough
-for Darby

Seger sang *Night Moves* on your car radio
while we rode round country burbs
blowing smoke out windows.

Do you remember telling me you missed
nights in Michigan, but chose to move
because the snow there was high enough
to touch a tall Indian's ass?

You told me that nights round here get quiet.
So quiet, you could hear deer chewing in your
garden. So quiet, you could hear
God calling his daughters.

Moon Ridge Drum Song

We could have hopped the train
to California, but the ties were broken

from the rails. And the only road out
is under water. And there's nothing here

but poke weed. Where once you took me
to the junk yard and pressed me hard

against the bones of a burnt car. Hidden,
with our jeans around our knees, pop 40

bleating from dead radios, I left this town
with you to California. I wrap our sick mothers

in blankets and place them in old cars.
And the only red light is for the sawmill.

And the poke weed grows, twists around
me to the side of the road. While planet

moon hangs above these woods where
in my dream, we drive away forever.

Chief's Two Left Shoes

You'd drink enough to piss yourself in your sleep
and wore two left shoes. You ate a can of Alpo
thinking it was corned beef, and started fights
with rednecks much bigger than you.

We made fun of you and joked you'd be dead
before your next birthday, but you said you knew
the future almost to the hour. You foresaw the fall
of communism and the Arab Spring.

You said we would be teleporting by 2015.
You said you could see clouds in our eyes.
How could you know I'd be the only one left?
I'm still waiting for my teleport machine.

I Don't Bless People When They Sneeze

because it's a stupid superstition left over
from the days when my soul could be snatched
from having my picture taken.

> Because you never see cowboys sneeze. Better yet,
> you never see outlaws blow their nose.

I don't know about you, but I don't need
to be blessed. It's not like I'll sneeze out
foggy dreams and old junk memories
of dancing at powwows jingle stomp jingle.

Damn, Joe, I might be in trouble from taking pictures
with so many white girls. Remember when we
used to eagle-call the number of feathers in our hats?

Forget their names, man. This year has been a thief.
I forget keys, birthdays, rent. Just you remember
in those pics, I'm the one with the shit-eating grin.

Crazy Horse never had his picture taken.
Crazy Horse kept a Kleenex in his war bonnet.

Portrait of a Velvet Indian Elvis

I've seen velvet Indian Elvis don a headdress
and scare the shit out of cowboys everywhere.
His suit dripped blood, his cape
was made of mocking bird wings,
a baritone highway pimp with a snarling lip.

Seen him sing and whole neighborhoods
become junkies who give away their babies
for a night with the King.

Seen him drive herds of buffalo through streets
of downtown Seattle, saving the souls of all the girls
who touched his braids.

Seen him sway to "Are You Lonesome Tonight"
with his arms spread like thunderbird
and his lightning snakes.

Seen him karate kick Coachella Indians in the nose.
Seen him rear back and attack
the entire Washington Redskins roster.

Seen him fall on his ass during a powwow
in front of 20,000 screaming "psychedelia"
into the mic just before cops took him away.

Seen him carve his own face on Mt Rushmore.

Seen him blow kisses to grandmothers
and play the blues at casino after casino.

Seen him stand in line at Walmart for diabetes meds.

Seen him sell food stamps for gas money.

Seen him die of a heart attack in a bowling alley

only to come back claiming to have had a vision
in which all half-Indians walk upside down.

Seen him sell his regalia as a centerpiece
to the museum of painted turtle shells
and living exhibits.

Seen him play charity baseball games
in his old neighborhood where he took the kids
to Dairy Queen and let them buy whatever.

Seen him pawn his guitar to pay the electric bill.

Seen him drunk on the fame of being the last of his tribe.

IV. Yakni hupia, Oka hupia

Stomping Grounds

"One year after the town was flooded, the city

invited Fats Domino to play a concert

where all the local musicians could play with him

and *your* grandpa wanted to play his fiddle with them,

but they said he wasn't eligible,

even though our family had been playing

music here since before 1492, so he

rosined his bow anyway and played

so hard that every Indian on the lake

came to hear him, and the entire police

force had to be dispatched to break up the great

Indian uprising of 1966."

The Great Flood

When the Sabine River was dammed to become Toledo Bend,
our half-blind grandmothers prayed to sunbeams.

When the town was flooded and St. Joseph's became a hospice,
our grandfathers packed dugout canoes with dishes and deer hide.

Portraits of Christ floated out from open windows, their brass
frames already corroding along cattle trying to swim to shore.

One generation later and bass boats bob in the channel.
Orange corks dip and jerk. Fish swim toward the sluiceway.

As children, we watched the water flow over the concrete weirs
and dared each other to touch the tainter gates.

Our mothers would call to us from the distance as we stretched
arm and leg over the water.

We ran when a boy fell in and got trapped in the spillway.

Helpless, I imagined him pulled into the vacuum, pressing against
the current. The endless looping, the panic

in his chest. His burning muscles
forcing him to take breath.

We listen for oars sloshing back and forth from history.

We hear how houses drown and boys disappear.

The town speaks of what used to be
and it's in the dry light of warm day

I know we've been dreaming.

One Artifact

You can find arrowheads in creek beds
and tar pools. Stone axes attached
to log trucks, feathers like red flags
whipping in the interstate wind.

Find coup sticks stacked with lumber.
                              Arrowheads everywhere!
Find one everyday
used as bookmark, fish hook,

tiger's eye, flint knife, obsidian
shovel-shaped incisor here,
a proud cheekbone there.
                              Skulls everywhere!

Easy enough to forget like keys
to grandpa's truck. Forget to replace
the busted radiator hose. Forget
family names. Saturday Mass.

The names for God (the one
followed after the dam) where we live.
Find spearheads in the middle of town.
The old town—the daube hut

with its carbon shadow burned
into earth. Forget how
to speak. How
to remember.

Elegy for a Drowned 1969 Camaro

They thought they could fly over the lake
into Texas for white women and Mexican
cocaine. Instead, they were found in the lake,
holding onto taillights, trying to lift the car
back on the road. They were making war
against America, then us, then their brother's
69 Camaro, primer grey with chrome mags,
now resting at the bottom of the lake. Tire squall,
night air, engine gallop. Their brother's car,
taking flight through red light after red light
until diving off Pendleton Bridge. So we sing
the death of our brother's Camaro, sunk
into history, into myth. *Goddamn Indians,*
only good one is a dead one.

The Parrie Boys Run Out of Gas in Norman, OK

"The old lady tells Larry he looks more Chinese than Indian, and when he says he's from Zwolle, Louisiana, she says, with her lips pursed, that it makes sense. He asks for a ride to the nearest station and she says there's an Exxon near Lake Thunderbird Reservoir and she'll take them, but first she wants to hear a song. So they pile out of the van, and before they set up on the side of the road, the old lady screams and speeds away, certain she was nearly car jacked by a bunch of Chinese Indians from the swamp."

Graduation Ceremony

You said it was a gift.
That, like you, I had earned
your trophy, wrapped in plastic,
cool and heavy as a rucksack.
It could have been the sawblade
helmet of Cortez, or Iwo's flag.
But it was your souvenir,
like foreign dirt, like a necklace
of ears, and as symmetrical
as the barrel of a Luger pistol.
My fingers traced the red field,
the black bent cross, and the twin
bolt patch that had been your enemy.
My face was a moving smudge
in the plastic. You were proud
I chose the Army. Now, sand fills
my shoes, and everywhere I go,
I leave dunes.

La Malinche Weeps

And tonight, thoughts of you take me back
    to the bar where you drag your cigarette
        and laugh at my stupid jokes.

      And for a few ticks of the cosmic clock,
  music howls to me from beyond the lake
you say we drown in every night.

This town is haunted by women
    who killed their babies
        at the beginning of the world.

      They swoop down and carry men
across the water and out of history.

Beast Kings, 3rd Infantry Division

In Baghdad,
fresh from a bombed out zoo,
elephants rooted through rubble
chasing lions away from soldiers.
And among blackening
bodies of militants scattered
in bone desert, Dumbo
trumpeted to Jumbo who trumpeted
a barrage of stumped feet
and ivory bayonets.

Gift Hour

The first thing you see is sun,
disc from sea,
flat as empty belly.

You say you are a survivor
as you go to place him under water
where deep grenadine clouds will spread.

And let's say you imagine gentle hands,
pull him away and out to swelling sea.

But maybe it's the tide pushes you back.
And your words leap from your tongue
and catch the wind like a kite

caught in salty air. Maybe it's gulls
and grackles' piercing caw changes your mind.

You touch him through thin skin,
running your hand over fist and foot,
ankle and tiny mouth.

You stand in shallows until the sun
fully rises red and then everything is red,
and you pray the only way you know.

My Father's Horses

Every year my father gets a horse.
Each marks another year sober.
Another year without the drink
and another year without the crash.

Each pony has a different name.
While others run all day and all night,
some just graze. With each new year,
I am further removed from the soured

sweetness of beer in my father's beard
that matted to his face like lake foam.
Like the scent of bodies who dared
whiskey only to end up slipping

into the throat of its current.
My uncles didn't make it.
All their lives they rode one horse
until it grew to leather and collapsed

into the river and drowned
in the hot nights of jukes, honky tonk
fist fights, and mornings in jail.
Every year my father gets a horse.

Each marks another year sober
and soon, he'll herd them out
of their fences and onto the plains,
100 mustangs kicking up dust.

Dry Summer Bone

The summer they drained the lake down,
we could see the old village, train tracks,
and graves the city swore had been moved.

When the mud hardened, we rebuilt the village
and replanted cypress and oak, and laid cedar
instead of sacrifice. The summer they drained

the lake down, got so low, suicides failed
to drown. They tried to pay us to pray for rain.
That summer when the lake was near gone,

our kids sprayed each other with water hoses,
sprayed water into sky so that it fell like rain.

Toledo Rez

Waves break from the bottoms
of power boats and glide toward
shore like rolling hills of fish.

Roofs of houses jut out
of lake as shards
where Indians, turned to fish, dance
in its belly like prize winning bass.

Indians dancing down there
have a brownness that hangs from
their bones like sacks of loot and corn,
like tamales and welfare, like whiskey
and crosses, and my grandmothers'
feet pounding mud dancing
cat fish dance while my grandfathers' sing
and swim through hollowed out cars
and trucks of flooded junkyard forests
of my ancestors.

Aluminum eyes pop up to watch
golden green waves rush beach like
foam fences marking border of an
underwater reservation.

They say when the lake was built,
all the Indians living there had to
learn to swim.

Our families have unstuck themselves from the trophy wall
that has kept them stuffed and cloud-eyed
for five hundred years.

They have pulled out the hooks and chanted
names of dead from the bottom of the lake.

They have stretched out their powerful fins and
crawled from the mud of Toledo Bend

without words,
without drums,
without songs,
without skins,

to tear through black tarry nights of oil fields,
to smoke sweet burning of the Marlboro man,
to sweat sawmills and end of piney woods,
to sniff the banks of Toledo Rez for Old Milwaukee
in the howling coon ridge night.

There's blood in the mud from the changing.
Over time, it will harden into clay;
a shard of pottery to prove
we were here at all.

**Thomas Parrie:** is affiliated with the Choctaw-Apache Tribe of Ebarb in west Louisiana. He is from Natchitoches, LA where he earned a B.A. and an M.A. in English at Northwestern State University. Parrie is also a graduate of the McNeese State University MFA program and has presented work at numerous conferences including AWP. His fiction and poetry has been published across various journals and his poem, "Dog Head Park" is a 2014 Pushcart Prize Nominee from *Codex Journal*. He was the School for Advanced Research's Indigenous Writer in Residence Fellow for 2018. Thomas writes and teaches at Southeastern Louisiana University in Hammond, Louisiana.

 **EL Kiki Shawnee:** is a young emerging artist from Oklahoma working in multiple mediums including paint/ink, beadwork, basketry, clay, textiles, and photography. "Nuestra madre, nuestra tierra/Ishki pim, yakni pim" **or** "Our Mothers, Our Land," is a multimedia work featuring original floral work and ledger art images of Choctaw, Apache, and Mexican women. These art images are set against a found map image of Toledo Bend Reservoir. Shawnee's mother is of Choctaw-Biloxi, Louisiana Creole, Freedmen, and Métis ancestry while her father is Quapaw, Shawnee, Miami, and Cherokee.